# What the World Cup?

by Bonnie Bader

illustrated by Stephen Marchesi

Penguin Workshop

For David—BB

For Louis and Dennis, both my brothers
and teammates—SM

PENGUIN WORKSHOP
An Imprint of Penguin Random House LLC, New York

Visit us online at www.penguinrandomhouse.com.

Library of Congress Control Number: 2018005174

ISBN 9780515158212                                    10

# Contents

# What Is the World Cup?

On June 21, 1970, more than one hundred thousand screaming soccer fans packed the Estadio Azteca. They were there to watch the World Cup final between Brazil and Italy. For the first time, two two-time World Cup winners—Brazil in 1958 and 1962, and Italy in 1934 and 1938—would face off.

This was also the first time that a World Cup game was televised in color, not in black-and-white. The Brazilian players wore canary-yellow shirts and light blue shorts, and the Italians, in blue and white, raced up and down the vivid green turf.

Twenty minutes into the game, Brazilian star Pelé headed the ball past the Italian goalkeeper. Brazil was up 1–0. Then Italy evened up the score. Tensions rose. But the Brazilian team was

strong. They dribbled and passed the ball up and down the pitch—GOAL!

Brazil was ahead by a point. Could they hold on to the lead? It looked that way. Five minutes later, Brazil scored another goal, making the score 3–1.

Then, a Brazilian forward in the left-back position passed the ball to a teammate who dribbled past four Italian players! After another pass, Pelé had control of the ball. Cool, calm,

and collected, Pelé passed the ball to team captain Carlos Alberto. Without missing a step, Alberto smashed the ball with his right foot into the corner of the net. Brazilian fans went wild. Not only had Brazil secured a victory, but the world had just witnessed one of the most beautiful and memorable goals in World Cup history.

# CHAPTER 1
## The Games Kick Off

Every four years, soccer fans crowd into stadiums around the world to cheer on their teams at the World Cup. Millions more watch the matches on television. The World Cup is the most-watched sporting event in the entire world.

Soccer, known outside of the United States as football, was first played in 1863 in England. Soon after that, a number of football clubs joined together to form the London Football Association. From that beginning, the sport quickly gained popularity throughout the world. Why? Because soccer is basically a simple game to play. All that's needed (besides players) is a field and a ball. Goals can be made from anything— garbage cans, cones,

even backpacks! But in official games, there are rules about the field, ball, and equipment the players use and wear.

In 1904, an international soccer organization called Fédération Internationale de Football Association, or FIFA, was founded in Paris.

**FIFA**
founded 1904

FIFA logo from 1977 to 1995

At first, just seven countries—France, Belgium, Denmark, the Netherlands, Spain, Sweden, and Switzerland—were members. Within a year, the number grew to fifteen after Austria, England, Germany, Hungary, Ireland, Italy, Scotland, and Wales joined. The heads of FIFA wanted to hold a tournament in 1906. But it never took place. Why? Because none of the teams sent in an application to play!

By 1924, FIFA had a new president, Jules Rimet. At the Summer Olympics in 1928, Rimet and FIFA's congress decided to try again to organize an international soccer match.

Jules Rimet

# The Pitch

Soccer can be played on either grass or artificial turf, as long as it is green. The field must be rectangular and marked by two short goal lines and two long touchlines. The center part of the goal lines contain the actual goals.

When the ball passes over the goal line where the goal stands, a goal is made. When the ball passes over the touchlines, it is out-of-bounds. The field is divided into two halves. In the middle of the pitch is a lined center circle. Opposing players can't enter it during the other team's kickoff.

Uruguay, which had won the Olympic soccer gold medal, was selected to host the first World Cup.

Some other countries in FIFA, however, weren't happy about that. Uruguay is in South America, and many complained it would take too long to get there. In those days, people still traveled by ship, which took a very long time. Another problem was the expense. Many players simply did not have the money to travel that far, even though FIFA promised to pay some travel expenses. Also, the European teams did not want

to lose their top players for two months—that was how long they would be gone!

As a result, some of the best teams—England, Italy, Spain, Germany, and the Netherlands—sat out. The organizers grew nervous. Were there enough teams to compete in Uruguay? Rimet stepped in and convinced Belgium, France, Romania, and Yugoslavia to participate. Romania's King Carol II handpicked his country's team and gave the players a three-month vacation.

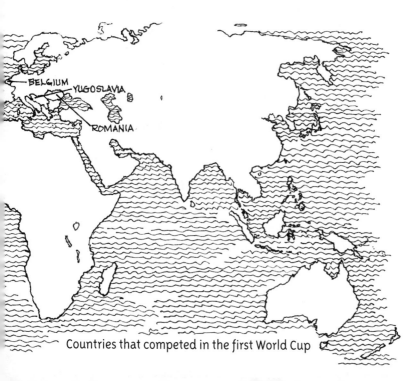

Countries that competed in the first World Cup

# What Is a World Cup Team?

Each member country of FIFA gets to put together a World Cup team. Every country has its own selection process, but in general, the players picked are the top in their sport. Athletes can play for the country from which they, their parents, or their family originated. So, if a player has lived in the US for five years, but was born in Brazil, he can play for either the US or Brazil, if selected.

In the end, with the addition of Argentina, Brazil, Bolivia, Chile, Mexico, Paraguay, Peru, and the United States, thirteen teams competed in the first World Cup.

In World Cup play, there are a series of games leading up to the final. On July 15, 1930, Argentina and France played in the second game of the World Cup. It was a tight match, with both sides controlling the ball well and defending their nets. By the time eighty minutes had passed, the game was scoreless. Then, at the eighty-first minute, Argentina's Luisito Monti scored. France was down by one and played even harder. Suddenly, the ref blew his whistle. The game was over. Argentina won.

But, not so fast!

The ref had made a mistake. There were actually six minutes left in the game! The players were called back on the field. Some had to rush out of the showers in the locker room!

But in the end, even with the additional time, France lost the match.

The final match was between two South American countries, Uruguay and Argentina. One of Argentina's star players was twenty-year-old forward Francisco "Pancho" Varallo. He had missed the semifinal game due to a knee injury.

# How Long Is a Game?

A soccer match is divided up into two forty-five-minute halves. The referee can add extra time for things like stopping play for injuries, but the clock does not stop as often as it does in American football. Halftime is no more  than fifteen minutes. If the game is scoreless at the end of ninety minutes, then two fifteen-minute overtime periods are added.

Before the final, Varallo was examined by a doctor who said his knee was too swollen to play. But the doctor was the son of Uruguay's president, and Varallo thought he was given a false diagnosis just so he wouldn't play! Varallo tested out his knee, which felt fine, and decided to play. In the locker room before the game, Varallo read some telegrams sent by fans, bursting into tears at the words of support.

Almost seventy thousand fans packed into the Estadio Centenario in Montevideo. Emotions were high. Police were called in to search spectators for weapons. They wanted everyone to be safe. As Varallo shook hands with his opponents at the start of the game, he was told that his knee would be attacked on the field. And it was. By halftime, he could hardly run. But he continued to play.

Many of the Argentinian players were scared when they took the field in the second half.

The Uruguayan crowd was growing unruly. And although the Argentine squad fought hard, they fell to Uruguay by a score of 4–2. Varallo later said, "From the best to the worst, everything happened that day."

The first World Cup was over, and it was a huge success. Now FIFA had four years to plan an even bigger and better tournament.

# CHAPTER 2
# Italian Winning Streak—1934 and 1938

Thirty-two countries applied for the next World Cup, and sixteen got in. Italy was picked to host, but then Uruguay refused to participate. The country was still upset that Italy hadn't played in their World Cup. So for spite, they withdrew.

Uruguay wasn't the only country unhappy about the choice of Italy. At that time, the country was ruled by a terrible dictator, Benito Mussolini. Many feared that Mussolini would use the World Cup to promote himself as leader of Italy. Sweden made a bid to host the tournament, but in the end it appeared that Italy was best equipped to play host to the tournament.

The first matches began on May 27 in eight cities in Italy, with the final held on June 10 in Rome between Czechoslovakia and Italy. Mussolini was there. Czechoslovakia scored the first goal, and the Italian fans grew nervous and angry. Mussolini just sat in the stands, in silence, staring at the players on the pitch.

Some say Mussolini had told the Italian coach that he would not stand for a loss.

In the eighty-first minute, Raimondo Orsi took a shot and . . . GOAL! And in the first five minutes of overtime play, Italy's Angelo Schiavio shot the winning goal. Once again, the host team had won the World Cup.

Four years later, the World Cup was held in France.

Once the participating nations were decided, teams competed for one of the sixteen finalist slots. Austria was among them. The only problem was that by June 1938, Austria no longer existed as a country. It had been invaded and unified with Germany.

As a result of this, Austria's best soccer players were supposed to play for Germany. But one of the top Austrian players, Matthias Sindelar, refused. Again, it was a question of politics. Sindelar did not support Germany's awful leader, Adolf Hitler.

Matthias Sindelar

# Adolf Hitler (1889–1945)

In 1933, Adolf Hitler was appointed chancellor of Germany. One of Hitler's idols was Benito Mussolini, and like him, Hitler made a successful grab for power, becoming führer (leader). Hitler's dream was to rule all of Europe. In 1939, World War II began after he invaded Poland. Hitler also hated the Jewish people so much that he wanted to have them all killed. He forced the Jews into concentration camps where six million were exterminated along with six million other people who were Hitler's "enemies." On April 30, 1945, just as Germany's defeat was certain, Adolf Hitler committed suicide.

The German team went without Sindelar. Less than a year later, he was found dead. Some think he was killed for his political beliefs.

Germany still had a strong team, even without Sindelar, and this pleased Hitler. But Mussolini was not about to let Hitler's team win the World Cup. According to legend, Mussolini sent the Italian team a very short but clear message: "Win or die." Some thought this message simply meant for the team to do their best, but others thought Mussolini wasn't kidding: If the team lost, they'd be killed!

In any case, Germany was out of the tournament early, losing to Switzerland 4–2. Even though a Swiss player accidentally scored a goal for the Germans, the Swiss scored four for themselves to put the German team away.

Italy barreled through the competition, but not without some unusual moments. In the semifinal match against Brazil, Italy's forward,

Giuseppe Meazza, was setting up to take a penalty shot when his shorts fell down! Keeping his cool, Meazza hiked up his shorts and knocked the ball into the net.

In the final match against Hungary, Italy won 4–2. After the game, the Hungarian goalkeeper—who had apparently heard the story of Mussolini's threat to the Italian team—reportedly said, "We may have lost the match, but we saved eleven lives." Little did he know that starting in a year, many more lives would be lost in World War II—lives of fans and players.

And no one knew that the world would have to wait twelve years for another World Cup match.

# CHAPTER 3
## The World Cup Returns

World War II finally ended on September 2, 1945. The very next year, FIFA started making plans for the 1950 World Cup. Brazil was going to host, which meant they had to build a new stadium in just twenty-two months. This stadium, the largest in the world, would have seats for 220,000 spectators.

Thirty-four teams put in applications, and fourteen qualified for slots. The other two went to Brazil, the host, and Italy, the previous champs. But when three countries withdrew, the competition was down to thirteen teams.

In the qualifying rounds, the United States was in a group with England, Chile, and Spain. After losing its first match to Spain 3–1, the US next faced off against England. Predictions were for a British blowout. In the United States at that time, soccer was not a popular sport. Unlike England, the US did not have a professional team—Team USA was made up of part-time players. But the United States players had heart. They took the field determined to play their best.

England fired shot after shot. But the US goalie, Frank Borghi, fought them off. Then, at the thirty-seventh minute, US midfielder Walter Bahr kicked a ball from twenty-five yards away.

The English goalkeeper saw the ball and got into position to make the save. At the same time, Bahr's teammate Joseph Gaetjens flew at the ball and headed it! The ball changed its path and flew into the net!

The English players were stunned. So were the fans. And that wasn't all. When the English couldn't answer the goal, they lost the game 1–0. The loss sent shock waves through the soccer community, especially England. In fact, it is said that some British citizens who read the score the next day in the newspaper thought that there was a typo and England had really *won* 1–0 . . . or even 10–1!

*Association Football*

## ENGLAND LOSES IN BRAZIL

Uniteo States 1. England 0

BELLO HORIZONTE. JUNE 29.

England was beaten 1-0 here today by the United States in pool B of the World Cup Association Football tournament. The Americans hung stubbornly on to the lead

Despite the amazing win, the United States lost to Chile in their next game and failed to advance. And although some might have hoped the win against England would boost American soccer, it did not. In fact, it would take another forty years for Team USA to qualify again for the World Cup.

Soccer did not need a boost in the country of Brazil—the Brazilians were crazy for the game and wanted a World Cup win! Brazil played the final match against Uruguay on July 16. Over two hundred thousand screaming fans packed the Maracana Stadium. Both sides played hard, and the game was scoreless at the end of the first half. But two minutes into the second half, Brazilian Albino Friaça Cardoso booted the ball into the net. GOAL! The crowd erupted in cheers. Confetti floated down onto the field.

Gunpowder exploded. Even so, the fans knew the Brazilians couldn't let up, not against a tough team like Uruguay.

## Soccer Positions

Each team has eleven players—ten out in the field and one goalkeeper stationed by the goal. The basic field positions are defenders, midfielders, and forwards or strikers. The defenders' job is to protect the goal. They try to keep the other team from scoring. The defenders have different names. The

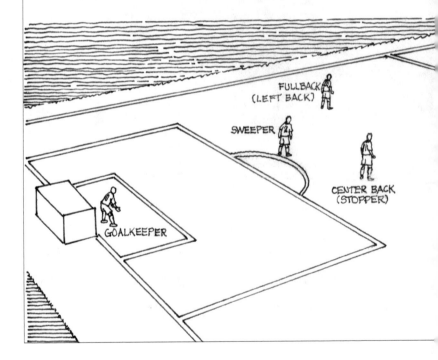

FULLBACK
(LEFT BACK)

SWEEPER

CENTER BACK
(STOPPER)

GOALKEEPER

center backs stay in the center, the sweeper stays back by the goal, and the fullbacks defend the sides. Some teams play with wingbacks who run the length of the field playing defense but also may attack. Midfielders link the offense and the defense. They bring the ball to the forwards and also try to stop the ball before it reaches the defenders. The forwards are the players who score the goals.

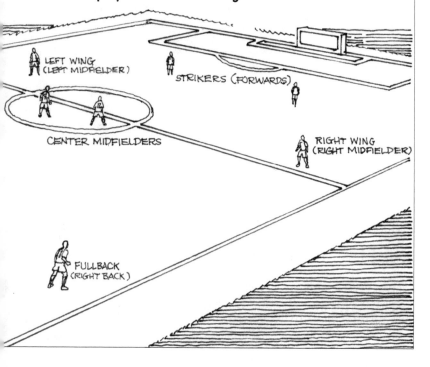

LEFT WING
(LEFT MIDFIELDER)

STRIKERS (FORWARDS)

CENTER MIDFIELDERS

RIGHT WING
(RIGHT MIDFIELDER)

FULLBACK
(RIGHT BACK)

At the sixty-sixth minute, Uruguay's right
winger, Alcides Ghiggia, dribbled the ball past
a defender and passed it to his teammate Juan
Schiaffino. Then—GOAL! The score was tied.
Now, with eleven minutes left in the game,
Ghiggia had possession on the right wing.

Seeing the defense out of position, Ghiggia kicked
and scored!

The stadium grew quiet. Everyone was
shocked. And the silence remained until the last
whistle blew. Uruguay won its second World
Cup, leaving Brazil, and its fans, stunned.

# CHAPTER 4
## Pelé

Brazil did not make it to the finals in the 1954 World Cup. Those games crowned a new winner—West Germany. The Brazilian team was still hurting from its back-to-back losses when the 1958 games, hosted by Sweden, rolled around.

But this time, Brazil had a secret weapon by the name of Pelé.

Pelé was born on October 23, 1940, in Três Corações, Brazil. His parents named him Edson Arantes do Nascimento, after Thomas Edison.

No one knows exactly when, or how, he got the name Pelé, a nickname he never liked.

From the time he was a young boy, Pelé was hooked on soccer. Growing up poor, Pelé had to make soccer balls out of old socks stuffed with rags and newspapers. He dribbled them wherever he went. At fifteen, Pelé joined Santos, a professional soccer club in Brazil. And as soon as he hit the field, he was a sensation! At the age of sixteen, Pelé was his league's highest scorer and was recruited to play for the Brazilian national team.

On June 24, 1958, seventeen-year-old Pelé stood on the pitch with his team, waiting to face France in the World Cup semifinals. France had crushed two of its previous opponents and came to the game with confidence. Yet, two minutes in, Brazil scored. France tied it up, but Brazil struck again with another goal in the thirty-ninth minute. Then, in the second half, Pelé shocked his opponents by scoring three goals, becoming the youngest player in World Cup history to do what is called a hat trick. The game ended with Brazil winning 5–2.

On June 29, about fifty thousand fans crowded Råsunda Fotballstadion in Solna to watch the

Swedish home team battle Brazil in the final. Thousands more were glued to their TVs at home.

At the end of the first half, Brazil was up by a goal. Then, at the fifty-five-minute mark, Pelé got the ball right in front of the goal. As Sweden's defense rushed at him, Pelé bounced the ball on his foot and sent it high in the air. In a flash, Pelé ran around the defenders, got the ball, and slammed it into the net. GOAL! Brazil increased its lead 3–1, and then thirteen minutes later made it 4–1.

But Sweden was not about go down easily. With ten minutes remaining, they narrowed the gap, 4–2. Then Pelé rushed toward the goal trying to meet a pass. He jumped into the air at the same time as the Swedish goalkeeper. Who would get the ball first? Pelé headed the ball over the goalie's outstretched arms and—GOAL!

Pelé collapsed to the ground, his eyes filled with tears of joy. Brazil won! Pelé's teammates lifted him up on their shoulders. And although the Swedes had lost, they couldn't help but admire soccer's newest superstar.

After the World Cup, Pelé received offers to

play for some European soccer clubs. But the president of Brazil had Pelé declared a national treasure. That made it legally hard for him to play for another country.

Pelé was again in the national spotlight for the 1962 World Cup in Chile. Even though he suffered an injury early in the tournament, Brazil went on to win its second World Cup.

The 1966 World Cup was hosted by England, and Brazil was hoping for a third win. But the opposing teams played Pelé hard—bumping, tackling, and tripping him any chance they got. He was bruised so badly that he couldn't play in Brazil's match against Hungary in the second round. Brazil lost 3–1, and later was knocked out of the competition. As for Pelé, he said he would never play in another World Cup game. He told a reporter, "Soccer has been distorted by violence and destructive tactics. I don't want to finish my life as an invalid."

The president of FIFA presents the first World Cup trophy
to the president of the Uruguayan Football Association, 1930

Uruguayan team and fans celebrate after FIFA World Cup win, 1930

Maracanã Stadium in Brazil, 1950

Queen Elizabeth presents the Jules Rimet Trophy to England captain
Bobby Moore after the World Cup final, 1966

England scores its controversial third goal during the 1966
FIFA World Cup final

Pelé (left) playing in a 1970 FIFA World Cup quarterfinal game

Italian player is tackled during FIFA World Cup final, 1970

Confetti rains down from the stands after Argentina wins
FIFA World Cup final, 1978

Pelé playing for the New York Cosmos

Italy's Paolo Rossi scores the first goal against West Germany in the 1982
FIFA World Cup final

Cameroon players celebrate during FIFA World Cup, 1990

Colombian defender Andres Escobar lies on the ground after kicking
the ball into his own net during a match in 1994

A player receives a red card, 1998 FIFA World Cup

Brazilian fans spell out the name of star player Ronaldo at the 2002 FIFA World Cup

Brazilian team celebrates its fifth FIFA World Cup win, 2002

France's Zinedine Zidane plays during the 2006 FIFA World Cup final

Protesters demonstrate in South Africa during the 2010 FIFA World Cup

South Africa supporters blow vuvuzelas at the 2010 FIFA World Cup

People gather in Brazil to protest FIFA, 2014

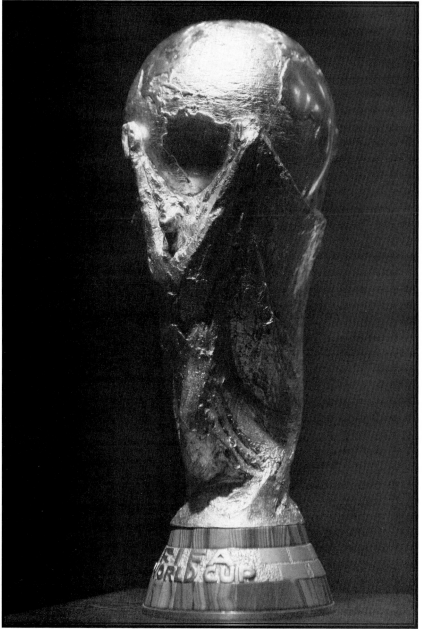

The current Men's FIFA World Cup trophy

Germany with the FIFA World Cup trophy, 2014

Although Brazil was out, the home team was still in—and they made it to the finals to face West Germany. The English fans sat anxiously in Wembley Stadium in London. Everyone hoped to witness the first World Cup victory for England, a country that treasured soccer. At the end of the first half, the score was tied. With thirteen minutes left, England's Martin Peters booted the ball into the net. GOAL! The fans went wild.

But then Germany's Wolfgang Weber took control of a loose ball and smashed it into the net. The game was tied and forced into extra play.

The teams fought hard. England's Geoff Hurst got a cross from his teammate, Alan Ball, right in front of the German goal. Hurst sent the ball flying through the air. It struck the goalpost and fell just behind the line. GOAL!

The crowd went wild, but was silenced a moment later when a linesman blew his whistle. The official said the ball had fallen in front of the goal line, disqualifying the goal.

The linesmen and the referee conferred on the field. The fans waited nervously in the stands. At last, a decision was made—the goal was good. But there was still time left. Could Germany come back? No. England scored another goal, and the final score was 4–2. All of England celebrated this first World Cup victory. Little did they know that this would be their last—so far—World Cup win.

By the time Mexico hosted the 1970 World Cup, Brazil had one of the strongest teams on the field, headlined by Pelé.

# Referees

On the field, the referee's word is law. If his decision is questioned, a player can face a penalty. Besides knowing all the rules, a ref must be good at dealing with people and be able to speak English and one other language. The ref must also be in top shape. A ref can run an average of twelve miles per game!

Yes, Pelé was back!

Although he'd promised never to play another World Cup, Pelé changed his mind after FIFA established the yellow-and-red-card system. Any player caught purposely fouling another player would be given a yellow card as a warning. A red card meant expulsion from the game.

Brazil faced Italy in the final and won 4–1, giving the country its third World Cup.

Pelé announced his retirement from soccer in 1974, but once again was pulled back into the game to play for the New York Cosmos in the North American Soccer League.

# Yellow and Red Cards

A *yellow card* is given to a player as a warning when he shows aggressive or unsportsmanlike behavior, disagrees with a ref, continues to break game rules, delays play, or doesn't respect the distance during a corner kick, free kick, or throw-in. *Red cards* are for more serious offenses. They are given for violent play, spitting at an opponent or official, denying a goal by handling the ball (except for the goalie), purposely committing a penalty to deny an obvious goal-scoring opportunity, using bad language, or after receiving two yellow cards. Once a player receives a red card, he is kicked out of the game.

Pelé played his final game in an exhibition in October 1977, between the Cosmos and Santos. During the game he played for both sides! He retired with a total of 1,281 goals in 1,363 games. To many, Pelé, who died on December 29, 2022, remains the greatest soccer player of all time.

# CHAPTER 5
## First-Timers and Repeaters

The year 1974 saw a change to the way the game was played. Up until then, players had a set position from which they rarely strayed. The defenders stayed near their net, the forwards were up toward the opponent's net, and so on. Now players could move anywhere on the field. If a defender wasn't near the opponent's goal, then a midfielder could run back to take his place. This style of play, known as Total Football, required players to know all the positions and be ready to move at any point during the game.

The 1974 World Cup went to West Germany, giving the country its second win. And in 1978, Argentina, the World Cup host, was crowned champion for the first time. In 1982, newcomer

Algeria joined the World Cup and upset West Germany with a 2–1 win in the first round. Going into the final game of their group play, West Germany had to beat Austria in order to advance to the next round. If not, the Germans would be out and Algeria would advance. The Austrians wanted West Germany, not Algeria, to advance; the way the standings worked,

Austria could not advance unless West Germany won. So they purposely let West Germany score. If the Germans beat the Austrians by three or more goals, Algeria would advance instead of Austria, and West Germany did not want to chance losing to the Algerians again. Austria was willing to advance the easy way and not have to face Algeria, whom they saw as a threat.

So the Austrians allowed West Germany to win that game 1–0. The Algerians were furious and protested. But it didn't matter. Algeria was out.

West Germany advanced to the finals and faced Italy. When the German team took the field on July 11 in Madrid, Spain, the fans booed. They were still angry over West Germany's unfair advance at the expense of Algeria. Italy was the clear favorite on the pitch that day.

The first half of the game was scoreless. Then Italy attacked. First Paolo Rossi scored, and six minutes later teammate Marco Tardelli smashed one into the net. Alessandro Altobelli topped it off with another goal. At the end of the game, the crowd was rewarded by witnessing Italy win its third World Cup.

The 1986 World Cup almost didn't have a host. The South American country Colombia was selected. But in 1982 the government admitted that it didn't have enough money to pay for the games. It costs a lot of money to build stadiums! So Mexico stepped in. Then on September 19, 1985, Mexico City was hit by a huge earthquake. Would FIFA have to find yet

another host? No. Amazingly, although this tragedy killed and injured thousands, the soccer stadiums were untouched. The Mexican government very much wanted to hold the World Cup to keep up the spirits of its citizens.

This World Cup welcomed three new teams: Canada, Iraq, and Denmark.

But Argentina, with its hotheaded star Diego Maradona, was the team to watch. His temper got him ejected from the 1982 Cup, in a game against Brazil. Now, Maradona was ready to shine.

Diego Maradona

In an exciting quarterfinal match against England, Maradona raced to meet a ball booted into the air by an English defender. At just five feet five inches, Maradona was short but fearless.

# Who Gets In?

In 1982, twenty-four teams played in the World Cup. And in 1998, the field grew to thirty-two teams. The road to play in the World Cup is long and complicated.

The host country automatically gets to play, leaving thirty-one spots. So, the approximately two hundred other teams that want to play have to compete in preliminary competitions. These competitions start two to three years before the actual World Cup! The competition is divided into six zones: Africa, Asia, Europe, CONCACAF (North and Central America and the Caribbean), Oceania (South Pacific), and South America. Before every World Cup, FIFA determines how many spots each zone will get according to the strength of the teams in that zone.

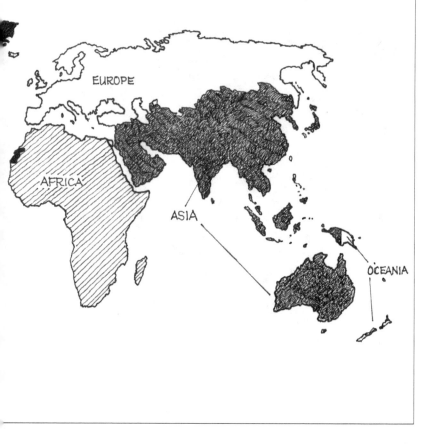

Maradona jumped into the air at the same time as England's six-foot goalie. Both men fell to the ground, and the ball slammed into the net— a goal for Argentina! Maradona jumped up in celebration. But Maradona had hit the ball with

his hand, a major foul. However, since there was no replay and the ref had missed the foul, the goal counted. Maradona later said that the ball went into the net by "the hand of God."

Maradona's strong play helped land Argentina in the finals against West Germany. The Germans were on Maradona's every move, making it hard for him to score. Then with six minutes left in the game, and the score tied at two apiece, Maradona made an amazing pass to teammate Jorge Burruchaga. GOAL! Argentina won its second World Cup.

# CHAPTER 6
## Red-Card Mania

Although the red-card rule started in 1970, no red cards were given out that year. In fact, throughout the 1970s and 1980s, no more than eight red cards were given during each World Cup. It was a different story in 1990. The 1990 World Cup, played in Italy, racked up sixteen red cards.

Why?

During this World Cup, the officials really buckled down on bad tackling and flagrant fouls. But that didn't stop the rough play.

Argentina powered its way through the tournament, shocking Brazil along the way. In the game against the host country, Italy, Argentinian Ricardo Giusti was slapped with a red card. The Italian fans were so upset with the rough play that they booed and jeered at the Argentines as they took the pitch for their final game against West Germany.

The rough play continued in the final match. Argentinian Pedro Monzon was the first player to be kicked out of a World Cup final. Later, teammate Gustavo Dezotti joined him in this dubious honor after tackling a West German player to the ground.

In the end, Argentina's rough play turned against them when West Germany was awarded a penalty kick and won 1–0. West Germany now joined the ranks of Italy and Brazil, with three World Cups.

# A Team with Heart

In the opening match of the 1990 World Cup, an African nation, Cameroon, shocked Argentina by beating the powerhouse team 1–0. Cameroon's excellent play was led by thirty-eight-year-old Roger Milla. Originally, Cameroon's coach thought Milla was too old to play. But Cameroon's president insisted that Milla be added to the team.

Although Milla wasn't a starter, he scored two goals in a win over Romania that helped advance Cameroon to the quarterfinals. It was the first time an African nation had advanced this far. Although Cameroon got no further, they made it into the hearts of soccer fans around the world.

# CHAPTER 7
## The World Cup Comes to the United States

The United States very much wanted to host the 1994 World Cup. However, FIFA said that

the US first had to develop a professional soccer league. Doing that would prove the country's commitment to the sport. The US agreed, and in 1996, Major League

Original MLS logo

Soccer was launched.

The World Cup was played from June 17 to July 17 in nine places across the United States: Palo Alto and Pasadena in California; Dallas, Texas; Orlando, Florida; Pontiac, Michigan; Chicago, Illinois; East Rutherford, New Jersey; Foxborough, Massachusetts; and Washington, DC.

PONTIAC

CHICAGO

FOXBOROUGH

EAST RUTHERFORD

PALO ALTO

THE UNITED STATES

WASHINGTON, D.C.

PASADENA

DALLAS

ORLANDO

The different venues meant playing in very different climates, from dry heat in Palo Alto, to humidity in Washington and East Rutherford, to extreme heat and humidity in Dallas and Orlando. Nevertheless, the matches drew huge crowds, an average of almost seventy thousand per game, which was amazing in a country where soccer wasn't yet that popular!

On July 17, Brazil and Italy faced off in the final match at the Rose Bowl in Pasadena. Each country had already won three World Cups.

# Major League Soccer

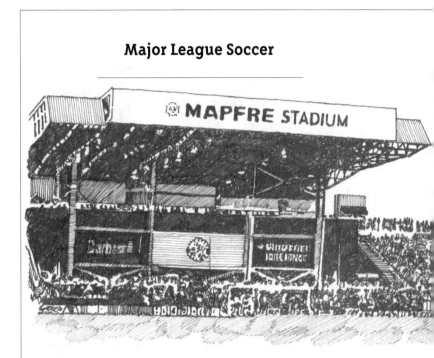

Starting a major league soccer organization in the United States was a major undertaking! Stadiums had to be built or reserved. Teams had to be formed. All this required a lot of money. In 1996, there were ten soccer clubs: the Colorado Rapids, the Columbus Crew, the Dallas Burn, D.C. United, the Kansas City Wiz, the Los Angeles Galaxy, the New England Revolution, New York/New Jersey MetroStars, the San Jose Clash,

and the Tampa Bay Mutiny. As of 2023, only five of
the original teams remained, but the league now has
twenty-nine teams (three in Canada), with plans to
expand. Major League Soccer not only helped bring
more attention to the sport in the US but helped in the
growth of youth teams. Today, kids all over the United
States play on soccer teams.

At the end of regulation time, neither team had scored. After 120 minutes of intense play, and for the first time in World Cup history, the winner would be decided by a one-on-one contest—the penalty kicks. Each team got five chances to score a goal by a player shooting directly at the net. Only the goalie defended. Whichever team scored the most goals on the penalty kicks would win.

Neither side scored in their first shots. By the end of the third round, the score was tied 2–2. Then Brazil pulled ahead in the fourth round 3–2. Italy's Roberto Baggio faced the net in the fifth round. It was up to him—he needed to score to keep Italy in the game. Baggio sized up the goalie, shot, and the ball flew over the goal. Baggio failed to score, and Italy lost. Brazil won its fourth World Cup!

# Rule Changes

Several soccer rules were changed starting with the 1994 World Cup:

1. Goalies could now only take passes from their teammates with their feet and not with their hands.

2. If a player dribbling the ball was fouled, and only the goalkeeper was between him and the goal, then the player who committed the foul would get a red card.

3. Up until now, refs called lots of offsides, probably the most confusing rule in soccer! When a player has the ball and is driving toward the goal on his opponent's half of the field, he must stay level with, or behind, the other team's second-last defender. Offside may also be called when an offensive player is "hanging out" near the goal, ahead of the ball and the second-last

defender, while a teammate has the ball. Now refs were told to ease up on this rule, and when they weren't sure if an attacking player was offside, they should keep the play going. In 2022, cameras began tracking the players and the ball, and this shortened the time needed to make offside calls.

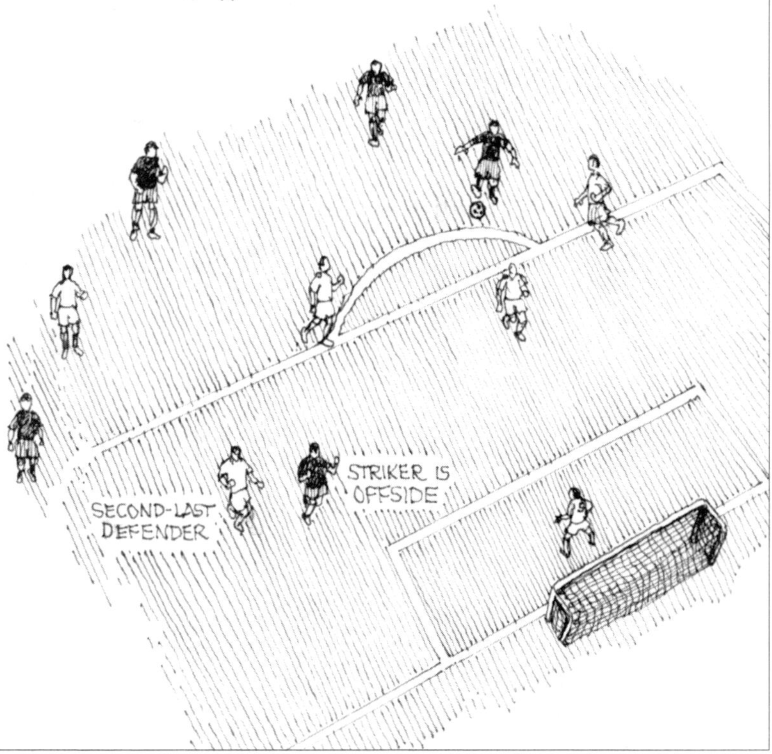

SECOND-LAST DEFENDER

STRIKER IS OFFSIDE

A team winning its fourth World Cup in a penalty shoot-out wasn't the only drama during this World Cup. First, Argentina's superstar Diego Maradona was thrown out of the competition when it was discovered he had taken banned drugs.

Then, in the United States' game against Colombia, Colombian defender Andrés Escobar made a terrible mistake. By accident, he kicked the ball into his own net and scored for the US! After that game, Colombia won a match against Switzerland, but it wasn't

Andrés Escobar

enough: Colombia had been a favorite to win the World Cup; now they were out. Escobar must have been both embarrassed and heartbroken.

Ten days after this mistake, Escobar was back home in Medellin, Colombia. He decided to go out with some friends. But wherever he went, people made fun of him. Mean-spirited fans wouldn't let Escobar forget.

Later that night, while Escobar walked through a parking lot, a man got out of his car. One witness claimed the man said, "Thanks for the goal." And then shots rang out. Escobar, the twenty-seven-year-old soccer star, lay on the ground, dead. What a senseless crime!

Medellin, and the rest of the world, mourned on the day of Escobar's funeral. More than a hundred thousand Colombians waited patiently to pay their last respects. Escobar had regretted his mistake, but he didn't wallow in self-pity. In fact, he had even written an article in a Colombian newspaper saying, "See you soon, because life doesn't end here." Sadly, Escobar was wrong. Soccer fans are very devoted to their sport, but everyone has to be able to tolerate defeat. That's part of playing any sport, not just soccer.

# CHAPTER 8
## Two Hosts and a Head Butt

Although the United States was riding high from hosting the 1994 World Cup, it did not advance past the first round in the 1998 games. France, which hosted the World Cup for the second time, won the Cup that year.

In 2002, the World Cup came to Asia for the first time, with two hosts—South Korea and Japan. They both spent tens of millions of dollars bidding to  host, and FIFA suggested the countries share the honor. At first, Japan refused, but then in time agreed. The hosts and the defending champion

# Old Foes

From 1910 to 1945, Japan ruled Korea. While the Japanese built new schools, roads, and railroads—the Koreans were stripped of their identity. In the 1930s, the Japanese even banned the use of the Korean language in schools and forced Koreans to adopt Japanese names. Japan occupied Korea until the end of World War II. Korea is now divided into two countries—North Korea and South Korea. Even though the Japanese were long gone by 2002, many people in South Korea still had not forgiven them.

(France) filled three slots, so twenty-nine spots were up for grabs. One hundred ninety-eight teams competed in the qualifying rounds.

The final match was played on June 30 at Yokohama, Japan. It pitted Germany against the four-time champs, Brazil. Brazil made it to the finals thanks to a goal by superstar Ronaldo Luís Nazário de Lima, who was simply known as Ronaldo.

Ronaldo

Ronaldo was born on September 18, 1976, in Itaguaí, Brazil. At twelve, he joined an indoor soccer team and was later signed by a professional club. Seventeen-year-old Ronaldo was named to the

Brazilian national team for the 1994 World Cup, but all he did was keep the bench warm!

In the 1998 World Cup, however, Ronaldo showed some of his amazing talent by hitting four goals and one penalty shot.

Even though he won the 1998 Golden Ball as the tournament's best player, Ronaldo was not in the starting lineup in the final match against

France. Why? According to a report, Ronaldo had a seizure the night before. After undergoing tests, Ronaldo insisted he felt fine. He was eventually put in the game but did not play well.

Now it was 2002, and Ronaldo was ready to play. And play he did, netting eight goals and winning the Golden Shoe Award as the Cup's highest scorer. Moreover, Ronaldo helped lead Brazil to its fifth World Cup!

Ronaldo returned to the 2006 World Cup, hosted by Germany. But he could not help advance Brazil to the finals. The final match that year saw two powerhouses, France and Italy, face off on the pitch.

Italy had all the ingredients to win: a strong defense, midfield, and strikers. France had Zinedine Zidane.

Zinedine Zidane

Zidane was born on June 23, 1972, in Marseille, France. The son of Algerian immigrants, Zidane grew up playing soccer on the city streets. At seventeen, he made his first professional appearance for France.

And in 1998, he scored two goals in France's 3–0 shutout over Brazil in the World Cup final. In 2004, Zidane was named best European soccer player of the past fifty years. In 2006, Zidane was thirty-three years old and was ready to help bring the Cup back to France for the second time.

On July 9, in Berlin, France took the field against Italy at the Olympiastadion. In the seventh minute, Zidane scored on a penalty kick.

And then Italy's Marco Materazzi booted a corner kick into the net.

At the end of regulation time, the score was still knotted at one apiece. Twenty minutes into extra time, Zidane sprang into action. But he didn't go after the ball; he went after Materazzi and head-butted him in the chest! The ref blew the whistle and slapped Zidane with a red card. Zidane was out! Zidane said he was egged on by Materazzi's insults, but the foul stood. France

had to play without their star. The game ended with Italy winning in a penalty shoot-out and bringing home their fourth World Cup. France was probably hurting from this loss, especially since it had had to go into the shoot-out without its star. But rules are rules, and Italy won fair and square. Sportsmanship—playing fairly and with respect—is a necessary skill to have.

# The Corner Kick

A corner kick is awarded to the offensive team when the defensive team kicks the ball out-of-bounds over its goal line. The ball is placed in the corner area and is kicked back into play. Sometimes a goal can be scored from a corner kick.

# CHAPTER 9
## Protests

In 2010, for the first time, the World Cup was held in Africa. The tournament, scheduled from June 11 to July 11, was to take place in ten stadiums in nine different cities across South Africa.

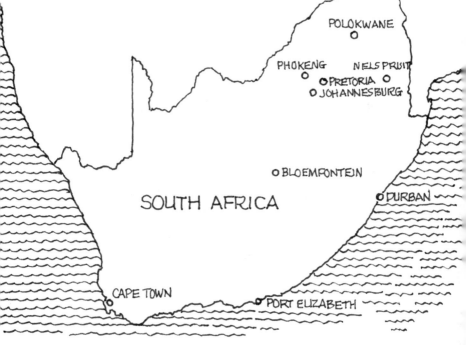

But thousands of South Africans opposed having the World Cup in their country. Why? Billions of dollars were spent building stadiums, while many South Africans didn't even have clean water, electricity, or decent housing. These protesters felt that their government cared more about soccer than its own citizens. Yet the games went on.

The protests continued throughout this World Cup, with heavy police presence not only at the stadiums but around the entire country. Did this have an effect on the home team? Maybe. South Africa did not make it past the first round—a first for a host country.

# The Vuvuzela

The vuvuzela is a long, brightly colored plastic horn, which when blown gives off a very loud noise. The vuvuzela appeared in the 2010 World Cup, and while fans had fun cheering on their teams with this toy, it gave others a big headache. Some called it an "instrument of torture"; others said it sounded like a "swarm of angry bees." It was banned from the 2014 World Cup in Brazil.

English fans also had a lot to be sad about during this World Cup. First, in a game against the United States, English goalkeeper Robert Green let an easy shot by US forward Clint Dempsey bounce right off his hands to tie the game at 1–1. Then, in a game against bitter rival Germany, Frank Lampard fired a shot that clearly bounced behind the line for a goal. But the ref said the goal didn't count! The disheartened English team eventually fell to Germany and were out of the tournament.

In the final match of the 2010 World Cup, Spain beat the Netherlands 1–0 in overtime, to take home its first World Cup.

The 2014 World Cup, hosted by Brazil, marked the first time that high-speed cameras were used to help the ref know if the ball really crossed the goal line. The decision to use this came after the botched call in the England–Germany game. With this technology, there is no need to stop the game to watch a replay. A signal is sent to the refs' wristwatches as soon as the ball crosses the line at the goal and flashes "goal" if the goal is good.

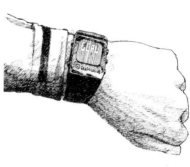

Cooling breaks, another first, were introduced due to the steamy Brazilian weather. Refs could call these breaks after the thirtieth minute of each half if the temperature exceeded 32°C, or 90°F. What a relief for the players!

But before this World Cup began, thousands of protesters marched throughout Brazil—just as they had done in South Africa. And for the same reason. The protesters did not think their government should be spending billions of dollars building stadiums. Instead, the protesters felt that the government of Brazil should use the money to improve public services such as education and health care. Other protests were to show support for the estimated 250,000 people who lost their homes to make room for stadiums. They hadn't been paid enough to find decent new housing. The protesters set fires, threw rocks, and carried signs reading FIFA GO HOME. There was a lot of sympathy for the protesters. Some Brazilians declared that they would not support their home team and would support another team instead.

The games went on, with Germany bringing home the Cup for the fourth time. Yet, the sounds of the protesters still rang in many people's ears.

Soccer, a sport loaded with fun and excitement, was becoming filled more and more with controversy. And it was about to get worse.

# CHAPTER 10
## Controversy

Early in the morning of May 27, 2015, Swiss police entered a hotel where a FIFA meeting was being held. Seven FIFA executives were arrested. The charge was that these officials illegally took money from television companies in exchange for picking them to show the World Cup on their stations. Television companies make a lot of money airing the World Cup, and there is lots of competition to get the rights to be the broadcaster. The FIFA officials were also accused of taking money to let some countries host the games. Later, more FIFA executives were arrested, and FIFA president Sepp Blatter was suspended.

People started to question if the hosts of the 2018 and 2022 World Cups, Russia and Qatar, had paid money to get the games in their countries. And if so, should they be disqualified and other hosts picked? But the games went on with the chosen hosts. Qatar was the first Middle Eastern nation to host. It was also the first time that the games were played in November and December, instead of June and July. And 2022 was the last time that thirty-two teams competed;

forty-eight teams will play in the 2026 World Cup, which will be jointly hosted by the United States, Canada, and Mexico.

# Women's World Cup

In England, women have been playing soccer since the 1890s. But beginning in 1921, the English Football Association banned women from playing on the same fields as men's teams. The sport, they said, was "unsuitable for females and ought not to be encouraged." It wasn't until 1971 that the ban was lifted.

The first FIFA Women's World Cup was held in China in 1991, more than sixty years after the first men's tournament. By 2019, the US women's team had won the Cup four times, more than any country! During the 2015 tournament, the US team played 540 minutes before allowing their opponents to score a single goal.

Hope Solo, goalkeeper for the 2015 US women's team

The choice of Qatar as the host country for the 2022 World Cup proved problematic. Once again, the chosen location was met with criticism—human rights groups were angered over Qatar's treatment of migrant workers (workers coming from other countries), as well as the fact that homosexuality is illegal in Qatar, which is an Islamic country. Thus, there was concern about the safety of LGBTQ+ fans coming for the tournament. The captains of many teams wanted to wear armbands proclaiming OneLove—a statement in support of the LGBTQ+ community. But would FIFA permit this? No.

Despite the problems off the pitch, the 2022 World Cup matches delivered plenty of thrilling moments, all leading up to a heart-stopping final between Argentina and France. Argentina's legendary forward Lionel Messi was playing in his fifth World Cup. At thirty-five, this was likely to be his last. And despite winning countless championships and awards, Messi had yet to lead a winning World Cup team.

The French team had many young superstars in the making, chief among them Kylian Mbappé. Although he got off to a shaky start in the final, by the end of the game, he had scored three goals. He was only the second player—after English player Geoff Hurst—to score a hat trick in a World Cup final.

Kylian Mbappé

The score was 3–3 at the end of four quarters, so the match winner would be decided by penalty shots. Messi and Mbappé delivered dramatic shots, but in the end, Argentina was victorious. The country had won its third World Cup, and a wildly happy Messi thrust up the World

Cup trophy amid thunderous applause and fireworks.

No other sports contest captures the world's attention like the World Cup. From the first

tournament in Uruguay in 1930, the World Cup has exploded in popularity—the 2014 World Cup reached over three billion people. And no other sporting event has such emotional ups and downs, from historic wins, to painful

Lionel Messi

losses, to the protests and controversies. Yet, through it all, the World Cup provides countless hours of electrifying entertainment and promotes national pride. The World Cup celebrates one of the most exciting sports ever known.

# The Winners and the Hosts

| YEAR | WINNER | HOST COUNTRY |
|------|--------|--------------|
| 1930 | Uruguay | Uruguay |
| 1934 | Italy | Italy |
| 1938 | Italy | France |
| 1950 | Uruguay | Brazil |
| 1954 | West Germany | Switzerland |
| 1958 | Brazil | Sweden |
| 1962 | Brazil | Chile |
| 1966 | England | England |
| 1970 | Brazil | Mexico |
| 1974 | West Germany | West Germany |
| 1978 | Argentina | Argentina |
| 1982 | Italy | Spain |
| 1986 | Argentina | Mexico |
| 1990 | West Germany | Italy |
| 1994 | Brazil | United States |
| 1998 | France | France |
| 2002 | Brazil | Japan/South Korea |
| 2006 | Italy | Germany |
| 2010 | Spain | South Africa |
| 2014 | Germany | Brazil |
| 2018 | France | Russia |
| 2022 | Argentina | Qatar |
| 2026 | | USA/Canada/Mexico |

# Timeline of the World Cup

1904 — FIFA is founded in Paris

1930 — The first World Cup is played in Uruguay

1934 — Despite some concerns, the World Cup is played in Italy

1938 — Italy wins its second World Cup

1950 — World Cup play resumes after a twelve-year break

1958 — Soccer sensation Pelé bursts onto the World Cup scene

1962 — Brazil wins its second World Cup

1966 — England finally wins its first World Cup

1970 — The yellow-and-red-card rules are established

1974 — Total Football, where players can play any position on the field, begins

1982 — Newcomer Algeria upsets West Germany in the first round

1986 — Despite a recent major earthquake, Mexico hosts

1994 — The United States hosts the World Cup

2006 — France's Zinedine Zidane gets tossed from the finals for head-butting

2010 — Thousands of South Africans protest the games in their country

2014 — Brazilians stage protests against their country for hosting the World Cup

2015 — FIFA officials are arrested on corruption charges

2017 — For the first time since 1986, US men's team fails to qualify for the 2018 World Cup

# Timeline of the World

1903 — Brothers Orville and Wilbur Wright complete the first successful powered flight

1933 — Nazis gain power after German elections; Hitler appointed chancellor

1939 — World War II begins

1950 — Korean War begins

1957 — Sputnik sent into space by the Soviet Union

1963 — Martin Luther King Jr. delivers "I Have a Dream" speech

1969 — Apollo 11 astronauts are first to walk on the moon

1971 — Voting age in the US is lowered to eighteen

1973 — Vietnam War ends

1980 — Former Beatle John Lennon shot and killed

1984 — Indian prime minister Indira Gandhi assassinated

1985 — Wreck of the *Titanic* found

1994 — Nelson Mandela elected president of South Africa

1999 — International Olympic Committee expels six members accused of bribery

2003 — Space shuttle *Columbia* explodes, killing all seven astronauts

2006 — Pluto is reclassified as a dwarf planet

2010 — 7.0 magnitude earthquake devastates Haiti

2017 — Donald J. Trump sworn in as US president in January

# Bibliography

**\*Books for young readers**

\*Christopher, Matt. *World Cup*. New York: Little, Brown and
    Company, 2010.

Fiore, Fernando. *The World Cup: The Ultimate Guide to the
    Greatest Sports Spectacle in the World*. New York: Harper
    Collins, 2006.

Lisi, Clemente A. *A History of the World Cup 1930–2014*.
    Lantham, Maryland: Rowman & Littlefield, 2015.

\*Petersen, Justin. *World's Greatest Sporting Events: World Cup*.
    La Jolla, California: Scobre Educational, 2015.